EXAMPLES *from* THIS BOOK

Who's who in this crazy pop group?

Activity develops ability to search text for relevant information.

Even the most reluctant reader will do this!

ELASTIC BAND

Mr. Trend has booked The Elastic Band to play at the Youth Club, but he can't remember which person plays what.

Can you help him? Look for the clues.

The Elastic Band were on the road again! They were in their van, driving to a concert. It was the first concert in their tour, so they were all a bit anxious.

'It's O.K. for you, Samantha,' said Chris. 'At least you don't have an instrument to worry about.'

'You can talk!' shouted Julie. 'You've only got four guitar strings to worry about — I've got six!'

The others laughed. But they still felt nervous. Mike had forgotten his cushion. He hoped he'd be able to find a comfortable chair to sit on while he played. You could tell Judi was nervous too. She kept tapping her drumsticks together in time with the windscreen wipers.

Two hours later they were on stage, ready to start.

Can you tell who is who in the picture? Write their names in the boxes.

Fun pictures to get the reading started.

Deductive reasoning is developed.

Challenging matching activity encourages attention to detail.

AUNT MAUD'S LETTERS

Maud has written to her five nieces — Alice, Angela, Agatha, Amanda and Annie. Ronald the cat has been playing with the envelopes and they're all mixed up.

Can you sort them out for her?

Draw a line from each letter to the right envelope.

Acknowledgements
The Bodley Head for the extract from
'*The present takers*' by Aidan Chambers
Eva Ibbotson for the extract from
'*The haunting of Hiram C. Hopgood*'

1

IN *this*

W e live in a world of words – being able to comprehend and make sense of what we read is an essential life skill. In Reading 3 a wide variety of activities encourages this understanding by promoting active and thoughtful reading. We seek, above all, to provide an enjoyable context for reading. It is enjoyment which is the key to improving the quality of reading. We have broken down the activities into three main areas.

USING READING

As children get older, the development of study skills which involve using reading becomes increasingly important. They need to be able to locate information quickly in a book and to search the text for the required details.

However, enjoying reading is equally important. Without enthusiasm for reading, children will not want to read a wide range of books. And this is vital for becoming a more confident reader. Some of the activities which encourage the use and the enjoyment of reading are:

The present takers on page 12 looks like an ordinary story in comic strip form. In fact it's a way of introducing a popular children's story for your child to read — just for enjoyment!

Ghoul End News on pages 15 to 17 is full of revolting details. It's about getting the main idea of passages, in this case newspaper articles, and matching them with the right headlines.

What a wedding day! on page 24 is a way of practising an important study skill – looking things up in a directory – in this case the 'Yellow pages'.

BOOK

WORD STUDY

Words are the basic building bricks of our language. It's important that they can be handled with confidence.

Understanding the precise meaning of individual words develops the ability to use them accurately and effectively.

Some of the activities which emphasise individual words are:

Elsie visits her relatives on page 20 involves choosing the best route for Elsie. This can only be done once the list of relatives and the list of places are both arranged in alphabetical order.

The cheat on page 23 is a 'proof-reading' exercise, which involves looking carefully at individual words and spotting mistakes. Teachers often encourage children to do this with their own work too!

Instant yuk! on page 31 is about choosing appropriate pronouns. The activity is designed to increase awareness of how words function. It takes the form of a dice game which leads to the making up of funny stories.

Sentences and "phrases".

Understanding the meaning of straightforward sentences is an important and basic reading skill; whereas manipulating phrases, for example similes and metaphors, is a more sophisticated skill. But both are vital steps towards a more confident handling of language.

Some of the activities which concentrate on these reading skills involving phrases and sentences are:

Marvellous metaphors and super similes on page 14 encourages an understanding of these kinds of phrases. Comic characters and situations are used to present and enliven a range of examples.

Beware Cousin Karen! on page 22 involves finding descriptive statements in a poem and comparing them with a picture to decide if they are true or not. It also reinforces the idea of similes.

The treasure of Dark Island on page 40 gets your child to read some sentence clues very carefully in order to assemble a map. No writing is involved, so there's no need to worry about handwriting or spelling in this one.

HOW THIS BOOK *works*

*Y*ou can share in the fun of **Success!** If you want, you can do some of the activities with your child. But **Success!** does not depend on you. One of the benefits of the range is to encourage children to enjoy working independently, not just when the grown-ups are around.

YOU

have a special role to play. It's the one that comes naturally to any parent: give all the encouragement you can!

If you can give your child the benefits of more individual attention, there is no need for you to *teach* specific skills. **Success!** does not require specialist knowledge.

WHEN

you're ready to start on this book at home, sit down together and go through it. Talk about the activities and the zany characters and enjoy the often crazy situations. Start one or two activities to get the feel of them.

Then help to choose an activity to be completed and say that you'd like to see it when it's done.

HOW

will you know things are going well? When your child is absorbed, *thinking* about the activity and really *doing* the work, then you'll know that progress is being made. Look at the back of this book for further guidance.

Speed isn't important. Enjoyment and commitment are the telling signs.

WHAT

should your response be? Praise the results – don't criticise. If you think there

is a better way of doing something, suggest it as an alternative, not as the only right way.

Make it clear that working at the activities is a good thing which brings praise. Effort does deserve recognition and it *will* bring results. Not least important, it will give confidence and increase enthusiasm for more activities and more learning.

Look out for opportunities to encourage work on other activities but go for short, frequent sessions – don't let it get boring!

Don't forget to *tick* off each completed activity on the *contents* page and share the sense of achievement and pleasure.

Success!

Reading 3

START HERE

I started this book on.................................

Name...

I finished it on ....

Pssst! It may look like a posh book but it's supposed to be written in — so do it!

Editorial and educational consultant

Dr. Roger Merry

ILLUSTRATORS:

Steve Brookes   Val Grace

Coral Calton   Matt Burke

M

Success! contents

> TICK ALL THE PAGES YOU'VE DONE HERE.

Reading Skills

WHO'S WHO?

We thought we'd tell you a bit about some of the people in this book. When you have read this page and have looked at the pictures, see if you can fill in the right names on the opposite page.

Maud can keep things under her hat, but **Elsie** usually lets the cat out of the bag.

Cannibal keeps biting off more than he can chew. **Mr. U** is like a bull in a china shop. **Myrtle** likes everything above board. Every time **Feetman** opens his mouth, he puts his foot in it!

Tatty Tricia likes putting a spanner in the works, but **Sid** goes over everything with a fine-toothed comb. **Weedy Weasel** is just a wet blanket. **Paul** is a chip off the old block.

Hatchet keeps putting the cart before the horse, and **Gus** is always barking up the wrong tree.

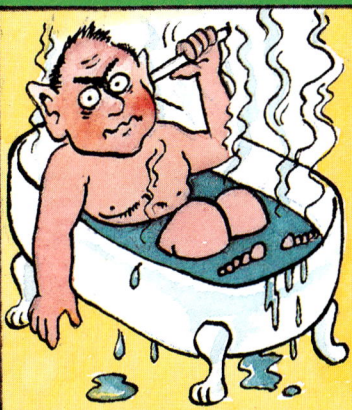

WOOF! WOOF!

Gargoyle is always in hot water, but **Skulk** keeps jumping out of the frying pan into the fire.

This is where you write the names. We've done the first one for you.

1.	Mr. U	is very clumsy.
2.	....	checks things carefully.
3.	....	keeps getting completely the wrong idea.
4.	....	spoils things on purpose.
5.	....	is always in trouble.
6.	....	keeps saying the wrong thing and upsetting people without meaning to.
7.	....	is good at keeping secrets.
8.	....	takes on too much at a time.
9.	....	gets things in the wrong order or the wrong way round.
10.	....	is no good at keeping secrets.
11.	....	keeps getting into worse and worse trouble.
12.	....	is just like his father.
13.	....	likes everything to be clear, with nothing kept secret.
14.	....	is feeble and pathetic.

You'll find the answers on Page 46

9

AUNT MAUD'S LETTERS

To Amanda

Birthday Wishes.

Miss. A. Smith,
13, Baker St,
LONDON.
SE3 9KP

Mrs. A. Jones,
27 Spa Lane,
BRADFORD.
BR3 XM7

9 Fir Street,
Snobville
7th May

Dear Annie,
Just a note to ask how you are. I hope your move went well. Moving can be so unpleasant. Do remember to take lots of exercise. I think living in big cities can be very unhealthy...

Mrs. A. Robinson,
'Sea View',
3 North St,
BLACKPOOL.
347 9KL

Maud has written to her five nieces — Alice, Angela, Agatha, Amanda and Annie. Ronald the cat has been playing with the envelopes and they're all mixed up.

Dear Alice,   Snobville
            I have   7th May
just written to your
sister Annie so I
thought I'd drop you a
line too. I do hope
she is going to be
happy in London,
it's such a noisy place
I'm sure you must
be glad you stayed

miss. A. Brown.
14, Bond St.
DURHAM.
DU 4 XL7

miss. A. Smith,
Elms Farm,
Budley,
Kent.
KY1SU

                    9 Fir St
                    Snobville
                    7th May
Dear Angela,
            Just a note
to say how much
Elsie and I are
looking forward to
staying with you in
June.
        I always enjoy
walking along the
beach, the sea
air always doe

            9 Fir Street
            Snobville
            7th May
Dear Agatha,
        Sorry I
haven't replied to
your letter sooner.
I have been so busy
organising the May
Day Fete. It rained
the entire day!
Elsie and I
got soaked

Can you sort them
out for her?

Draw a line from each letter to
the right envelope.

The present takers

Lucy - Beware.
Melanie Prosser
- she is out to
get you
Angus xxx

2.
Bye, mum, see
you after school.

Wait here. Then
we won't miss he

I'll put her in
an armlock.

4. Angus is a bit in love with Lucy. He wants to protect her. But he's afraid of what the teachers will do if he attacks the girls.

We'll get her behind the cycle shed.
Be all smarmy smiles
till then.

5. Mrs. Harris, the teacher, tells Angus to come inside. The three bullies will be able to get Lucy now!

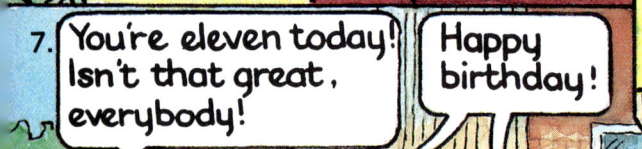

7. You're eleven today!
Isn't that great,
everybody!

Happy
birthday!

8. No one goes to help Lucy. They are too afraid of the school bullies.

Let me go!

3. *Meanwhile . . .*
Melanie Prosser, Sally-Ann Simpson and Vicky Farrant are waiting for Lucy. It is Lucy's birthday. But they are not waiting to give her presents. These three girls are the school bullies . . .

6. Until this moment Lucy has pretended to herself that she will be safe. It won't happen. Not to her.

Friends of yours?

Same class.

Lucy is helpless. It's three against one. t can Angus help her?

Leave my things alone.

Shut up, Whining Winnie.

10.

Running feet echoed round the shed. Angus burst into view, skidding to a stop by the corner. He glared at the little group frozen into statues by his arrival. But the hair closed over his face at once. Melanie stood up, glaring back. 'Had an eyeful?' she said, hands on hips.

'Leave her alone,' Angus said unimpressively.

'What's it to you, you hairy beanpole?' Sally-Ann said. She had a voice that sliced your ears when she wanted it to.

'Just leave her, that's all.'

'He do fancy her,' Vicky said, matter-of-fact.

'Oooo d' you think so!' Sally-Ann hooted.

'No I don't!' Angus said too quickly.

'Yes you do,' Melanie said, not even smiling. 'Well, you needn't worry. We're only talking. No harm in talking, is there? So you can just bug off, Angus Burns, because what we're having with your sweetheart,' she paused, challenging him, 'is a private conversation.'

There was silence. Angus opened his mouth, then shut it. He looked sideways as if someone out of sight round the corner were talking to him.

'Have you got some of your stinky friends with you'? Sally-Ann shouted. 'They don't scare us. You know what'll happen if we tell Mr. Hunt you boys have been bothering us girls.'

Angus shifted on his feet, looking back and away. Finally he brushed the hair out of his face and said, 'Just watch it, Prosser, that's all.'

'I'd rather not watch your ugly mug at all, if you don't mind,' Melanie said. 'Yuk! Put your hair over it again!'

'I'm warning you,' Angus said, straining against his anger.

'Don't forget old Hunt,' Melanie said.

Angus hesitated; then, seething, slowly backed away round the shed corner.

What will happen to Lucy now? You can find out by reading 'The present takers' by Aidan Chambers. You could borrow this book from the library or ask your mum or dad to buy it for you from the local bookshop. You can cut out the bit about the book and take it with you.

The present takers
A. Chambers
Bodley Head,
1983

Marvellous metaphors

Metaphors say one thing but really mean something else.
Can you match the metaphors? Draw a line between each metaphor and its real meaning.

She let me off the hook.

He is always picking holes in my work.

She dropped me right in it.

My teacher keeps criticising what I do.

My friend made me take the blame.

My teacher didn't punish me at all.

What do these metaphors really mean? **Write here.**

I want to pick your brains.

I'm over the moon.

I'm letting off steam.

1. ....

2. ....

3. ....

1.

2.

3.

and super similes

Similes are like metaphors except they always include the word 'as' or 'like'.

My mum's got a a memory like a sieve.

Oh no, I haven't.

Can you make up some similes?
Try to complete each of these.

as slippery as ....

as wriggly as ....

as terrifying as ....

as sick as ....

as hard as ....

as disgusting as ....

as .... as a jelly.

as .... as Skulk's trousers.

These metaphors and similes are mixed up. *Put a 'm' by those you think are metaphors and 's' by the ones you think are similes.*

The news spread like wildfire. ....

We were like two ships passing in the night. ....

He gave a dazzling performance. ....

I am hungry for information. ....

I am as blind as a bat. ....

Ugghh!

14

THE GHOUL END NEWS

What have you been doing, Skulk? Where are all the stories for the next edition of Ghoul End News?

I really fancied some paper to go with the fried worms and mayonnaise in my sandwich. It's all right, I haven't eaten the sandwich yet. I'll just get the pieces out.

On the next page you'll find page 2 of the next edition of the Ghoul End News. Skulk only left the headlines when he cut out the stories. On page 17 are the missing stories — Skulk's cleaned most of the worms off! *Can you cut them out and fit them in the right place in the newspaper?*

GRUDS' is a made up word. Can you guess what gruds really are? Here are some clues.

Now where did I put the gruds I bought you, Maud?

Gruds are made to be licked.

Gruds come in all different colours.

Some gruds are very valuable.

People buy extra gruds near Christmas time.

You can buy first-class gruds and second-class gruds.

THE GHOUL END NEWS

Fresh squid brings a damper

A New Recruit?

More blood needed

Former Star in fishing tragedy

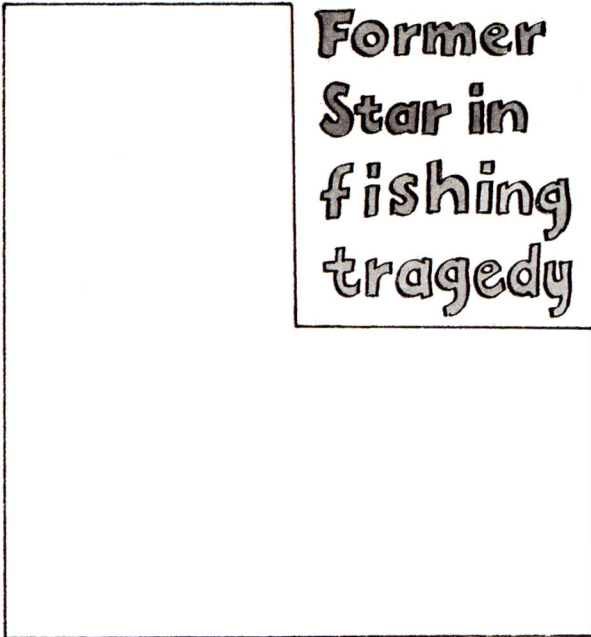

Guest House Owner in Siege Drama

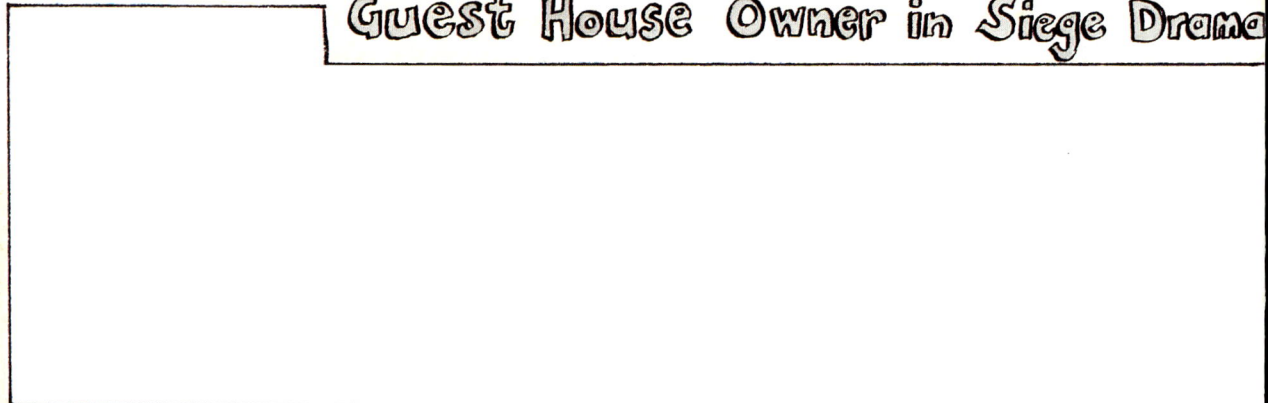

A fishmonger in Bone Street was fined by magistrates under the Trade Descriptions Act for selling 'stale squid' that was too fresh. J.R. Shark said in his defence that they seemed smelly enough to him. He later admitted that he did have a cold at the time. Mr. Shark was said to be very upset.

Police reinforcements have arrived in Ghoul End. But local villains can heave a sigh of relief. It will be some time before this new recruit starts on the beat. Here is P.C. Skull Junior trying on his dad's cap for size. He doesn't seem too happy about it. Shortly after this picture was taken P.C. Skull was taken to hospital suffering from severe neck injuries.

The ghoul drowned last week while fishing Bog Park pond has been identified as the former star of the long running T.V. serial 'Ghoulbusters', J.D. Freake played the part of the landlord of 'The Ghoul Arms'. He leaves a widow, two baby ghouls and a 20 foot long pet python. His widow said yesterday, 'I am only grateful that my husband didn't take the python with him.'

A guest house owner was held hostage today by an irate customer who complained that there was not enough mould on his brain pie. Police were called in when G. Grot, a twenty-five-year-old unemployed ghoul from 6, Skull Close, refused to loosen his grip on the owner's throat. The guest house owner, C. Gargoyle, said that his brain pie was the mouldiest in the whole of Ghoul End.

Pints of blood have been disappearing from the local hospital. Thirsty football fans from the adjoining football ground are thought to be responsible. More blood is urgently needed and all local vampires have been asked to collect as much as they can. The local council is to meet on Tuesday to discuss building a ditch between the hospital and the football ground.

17

FIND THE FLAGS

Here are the flags of six different countries. But which is which?

Can you sort them out? Here are some clues.

* The Austrian flag is orange and white.

* The Spanish flag has three stripes but only two colours.

* The Austrian flag has three stripes.

* The Indonesian flag has the same two colours as the Austrian one.

* The flag of Monaco is one of the first three.

* The flag of Colombia has a yellow stripe.

* The Netherlands flag has red and blue but no yellow.

Can you colour in these blank flags correctly? You'll find the answer on page 46.

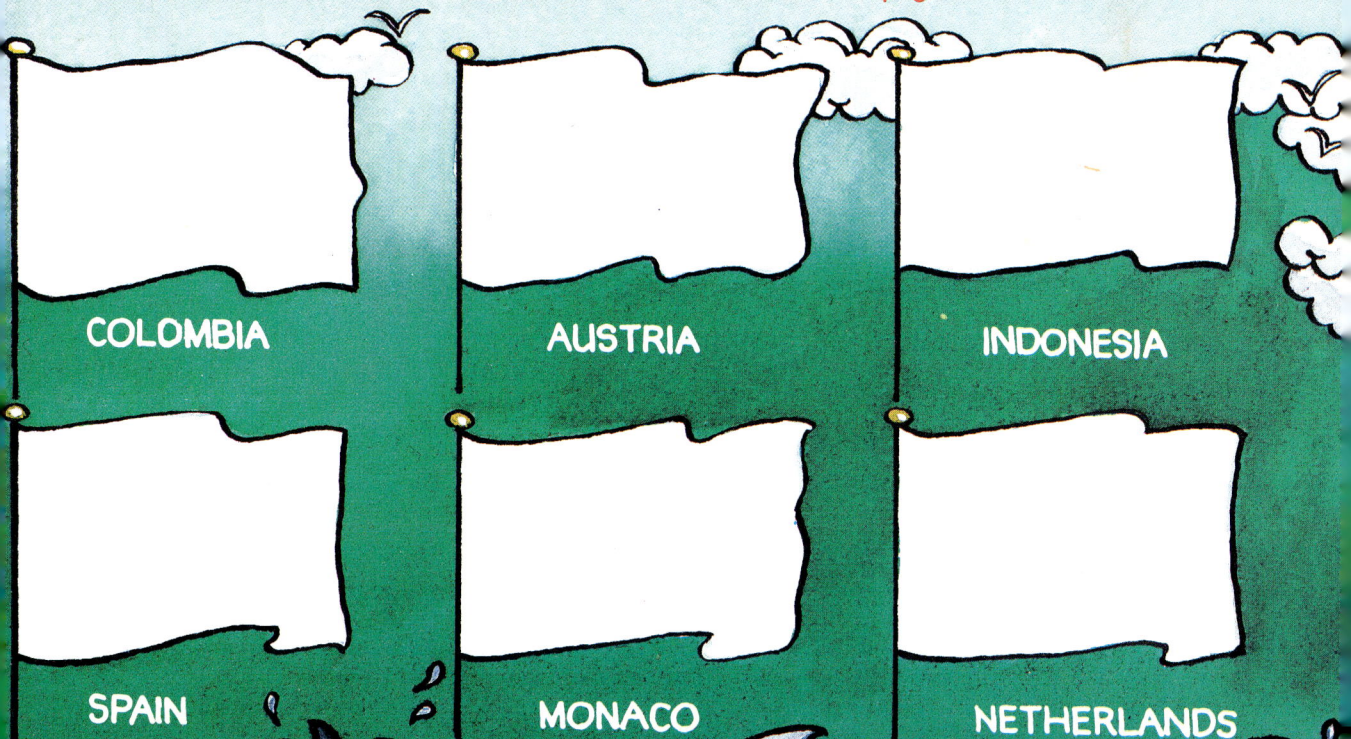

COLOMBIA

AUSTRIA

INDONESIA

SPAIN

MONACO

NETHERLANDS

Elsie visits her relatives

Aunt Evelyn will be furious if I see Elizabeth before seeing her – and Edward always wants to be last so that he can hear the gossip about everybody else. What can I do, Maud?

See them in alphabetical order, Elsie, then no-one will be upset.

Should I put the people or the places in alphabetical order?

Which ever would be quicker, my dear.

Elsie has decided to take her bicycle and Ronald the cat to visit all her relatives. They live all over the country and she can't decide in which order to see them.

Can you help Elsie work out the quicker route? First write the names of the people in the boxes on the map. Then draw two routes on the map, one putting the places in alphabetical order, the other putting the names of the people in alphabetical order. Which would be quicker?

Here are the people Elsie has to see:

Cousin Elizabeth lives in Birmingham.

Niece Ellen lives in Bangor.

Brother Edward lives in Barnstaple.

Brother Eric lives in Bolton.

Sister Elspeth lives in Blackpool.

Nephew Ernie lives in Bradford.

Great-niece Emma lives in Braemar.

Cousin Esther lives in Brighton.

Aunt Evelyn lives in Bournemouth.

Brother Egbert lives in Bath.

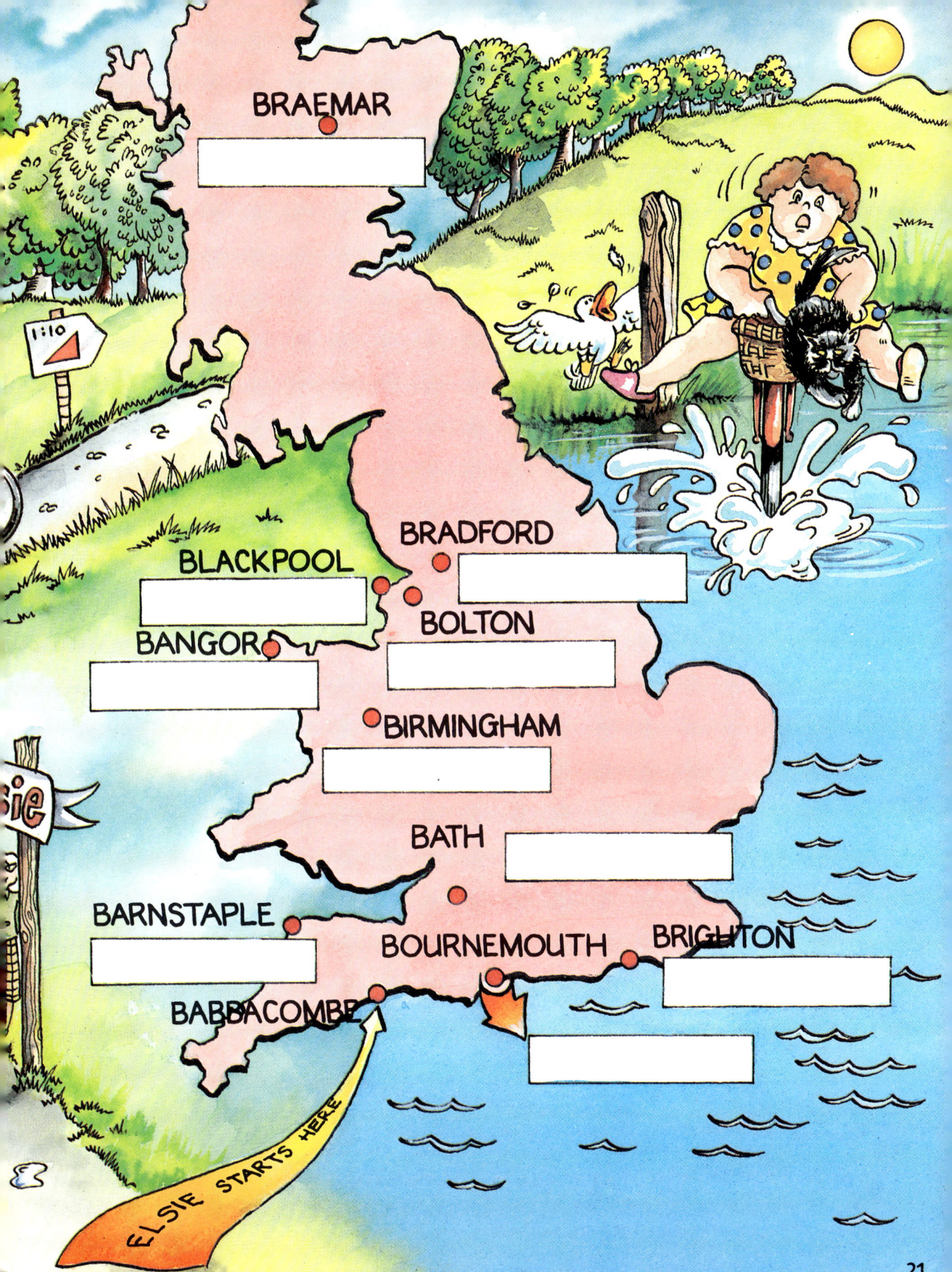

BRAEMAR

BRADFORD

BLACKPOOL

BOLTON

BANGOR

BIRMINGHAM

BATH

BARNSTAPLE

BOURNEMOUTH

BRIGHTON

BABBACOMBE

ELSIE STARTS HERE

1:10

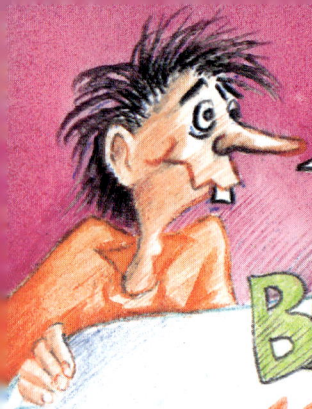

BEWARE cousin Karen!

My cousin Karen is a scruffy little girl,
Noisy as a tot and windy as a whirl,

Hair like a hedgehog, nose like a bee,
Mouth like a caterpillar swimming in tea.

Won't wash her face, won't clean her teeth,
Eyes like a big wolf's baying on the heath.

Wears big earrings and long red skirts,
Thinks she's beautiful, and always flirts.

Won't wear spectacles, won't wear socks,
Hates striped pyjamas. Fists like rocks.

Skinny as a beanpole, bony as a rake,
Lives on chewing gum and coconut cake.

So beware cousin Karen, with tattoos on her arm:
If she's coming down your way — SOUND THE ALARM!

Do you know what Karen says about me?
'Your muscles are of jelly and your brain is just a pea.'

Pah! Wait till she visits me late next week.
I'll show her this poem. She'll hate the cheek!

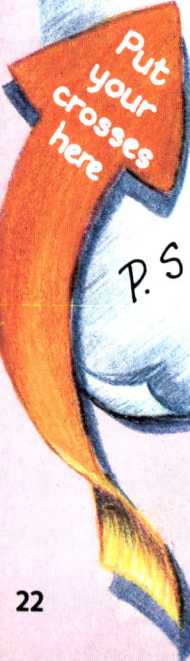

P.S.

Put your crosses here

Here is what Karen really looks like.

Weedy Weasel said many things about her which aren't true. **Can you put a cross by the side of those lines where Weedy has made a mistake? If there are two mistakes on one line, then put two crosses. How many things are there wrong altogether?** Find out if you are right on page 46.

22

The Cheat

Presses roll in 15 minutes

THE EDITOR

Here are the marks to use.

This is a newspaper article for *The Daily Globe*. Before the newspaper is printed all the stories have to be checked for printing mistakes. The person who does this is called a proof reader. They use special marks. For each mistake they make one mark in the margin and one on the writing itself.

You are now the proof reader for The Daily Globe. You have to read this article and mark all the mistakes. The editor says everything must be ready for printing in 15 minutes. Can you find them all in time?

MEANING	MARGIN MARK	MARK IN WRITING
change to capital letter	caps	–(under the letter to be changed)
Something left out or spelling mistake	∧(and missing item or correct spelling)	∧(through or between words)
change from capitals to small letters (lower case)	l.c.	◯(round letter to be changed)
take out words or letters	♪	–(cross out word or letters to be changed)

We've marked the first two mistakes, to give you the idea.

The cheat

In 1904 the olympic Games were held in St. Louis, U.S.A. It was the day of the marathon. Among the runners∧ an American called fred Lorz. The runners in this race Have to cover 26 miles though the town and country before they finish in the stadium itself. it was very hot. The runners found hard going. Of the 31 entries 17 dropped dropped out. Fred Lorz exhausted. He dropped out after 14 kilomettres The rest carried on. Their was excitement in the stadium. The winner have been sighted. As he came onto the Track the crowd yelled with delight. He wore the colours of U.S.A. It was Fred Lorz!

How had he done it The crafty Fred had hitched a lift in a car. The truth soon came out out and Fred was disqualified. Fortuntely for the Americans another of there countrymen came next so they got the gold after all! it still must have taken some time to get over the shame of Fred!

Caps
∧was

You'll find all the 20 mistakes marked on page 46.

WHAT A WEDDING DAY!

Augustus Broadbent shouted for help. He's heard the saying 'pigs might fly' but he had never expected to find one crashing through his roof! It had fallen right through the tiles and now it was halfway through the bedroom ceiling.

What a day for it to happen. It was the day that Augustus had planned to get married and there was so much to do! The cooker had broken and he couldn't make the pies for the reception. He still had to find a photographer.

His sister, Anastasia Appleby, couldn't hear him shouting. She was in the garage, trying to get the car to work. She was being deafened by the sound of the radio — she just couldn't get it to switch off. Where could she get a new gearbox at this time of day? How were they going to get to the church, if the car wouldn't start?

'Augustus!' she called. 'We are going to have to get on the telephone and get help.'

Augustus and Anastasia have a lot of problems. You've read about some. The picture shows more.

Who can they find to take the pig away?
Will they need a crane?
Where would they get it from?
Who will mend the roof?

You could make a list of all their problems, like the one we've started here. You might need a separate piece of paper. Then find your local 'Yellow Pages' telephone directory and write down the names and telephone numbers of the businesses which might be able to help.

Problem.	Who to telephone (use your Yellow Pages)
Oven broken - can't make pies!	Crumbles Bakery . 8951
Hole in roof.	
Pig to be taken away.	

MURDER AT MELFORD HALL

THE CRIME

Who killed the Colonel?

Colonel Murphy was murdered on Friday evening. The butler, Alfred Jones, discovered the body on the floor of the study at 6.20 p.m. He immediately phoned the police. Inspector Moose and Detective Sergeant Peabrain arrived at 6.35 p.m. They found an empty sherry glass beside the body.

This smells of arsenic – now who would want to poison the Colonel?

THE SUSPECTS

Four people had arrived that Friday afternoon to stay for the weekend. They were:

William and Clara Butterfield
William had recently become a friend of the Colonel. This is the first time Clara has met the Colonel. When she saw him she knew immediately that he was the same man who, 40 years earlier, had killed her son in a driving accident. He had been convicted of reckless driving but had got off with a small fine. She had told her husband as soon as they went upstairs to unpack.

Dr. James Crombie
James Crombie has been a friend of the Colonel for many years. They both belong to the same golf club. James is treasurer. The Colonel has recently discovered that James is taking club funds to pay off some gambling debts.

Emma Seaton
Emma is the Colonel's niece. Many years earlier she had been engaged to be married. Her boyfriend was in the Colonel's regiment. The Colonel had accused him of an offence that he did not commit. Ten years ago to the day the young man had shot himself.

Also living in the house with the Colonel were:

Alfred and Mary Jones
Alfred and Mary have worked for the Colonel for 15 years. Mary does all the cooking. The Colonel has recently told them to leave as he believes Alfred has been stealing cigars.

I want to take statements from everyone in the house. Make sure no-one leaves, Peabrain!

The Statements

Alfred Jones

1. At 6 p.m. I took a tray with five glasses and some sherry to the drawing room.

2. I gave each of the guests a glass of sherry. The Colonel took his drink to the study. He said that he had an urgent letter to write to the Chairman of the Golf Club.

3. I returned to the kitchen where my wife was busy preparing the dinner.

4. At 6.20 p.m. I went to the study to ask the Colonel about seating arrangements for dinner. I found him lying dead on the floor.

William Butterfield

1. Let me see . . . it must have been about 6 p.m. when Jones brought us all a sherry. Colonel Murphy said he had to finish a letter and left us.

2. Clara was in a bit of a state, but she asked Emma to go with her into the garden, so I said I would join James for a game of billiards before dinner. First I had to nip upstairs and fetch a book I'd promised to lend Emma.

3. I met Emma at the bottom of the stairs and gave her the book.

4. Then James and I played billiards. I was doing rather well — then all of a sudden Jones burst in and said the Colonel was dead. What a shock!

Dr. James Crombie

1. Poor old fellow — who would want to murder Harry? We've been friends for years you know. Well, at 6 p.m. we were all in the drawing room and Jones brought us all a drink. I would have liked a gin and tonic to be honest, but Harry only ever serves sherry.

2. When I'd finished my drink I asked William to join me for a game of billiards. I'd never met him before, but he seems a nice enough fellow.

3. While I was waiting for William I practised a few shots.

4. Then William joined me and we began to play. He was a bit too good for me.

Emma Seaton

1. But this is terrible! Uncle Harry murdered in his own house. I'll try to help you, Inspector, but you do understand how upset I am, don't you? We'd all had a glass of sherry, then Clara asked me to show her the garden.

2. It was a chilly evening so I said I would pop upstairs to get a sweater.

3. I met William at the bottom of the stairs and he gave me a book which he had promised to lend me — I read a lot you know — what else is there to do?

4. When I had got my sweater I joined Clara in the garden — we were just walking across the lawn when William came tearing out of the house to tell us about Uncle.

Mary Jones

1. I didn't leave the kitchen at all. The Colonel just doesn't realise how much extra work it is when he has guests. An ungrateful man, he is.

2. After he'd taken in the sherry, Alf came in and helped with the dinner.

1. When I had realised who Harry Murphy was I certainly felt like killing him. But William had told me to stay calm and behave normally. We all had a drink in the drawing room. The Colonel took his drink off to the study.

2. I needed some fresh air so I asked Emma if she would show me the garden. She said that she would get a sweater first.

3. I waited for her on the terrace.

4. When she came out we walked across the lawn.

If you read the statements you will see that everyone in the house was on their own for a few minutes between 6 p.m. and 6.20 p.m. Any one of them would have had just enough time to visit the Colonel in his study and to slip some arsenic into his glass.

Look carefully at this plan of Melford Hall, and at the pictures. Somebody is lying. That person is the murderer. There is one important clue.

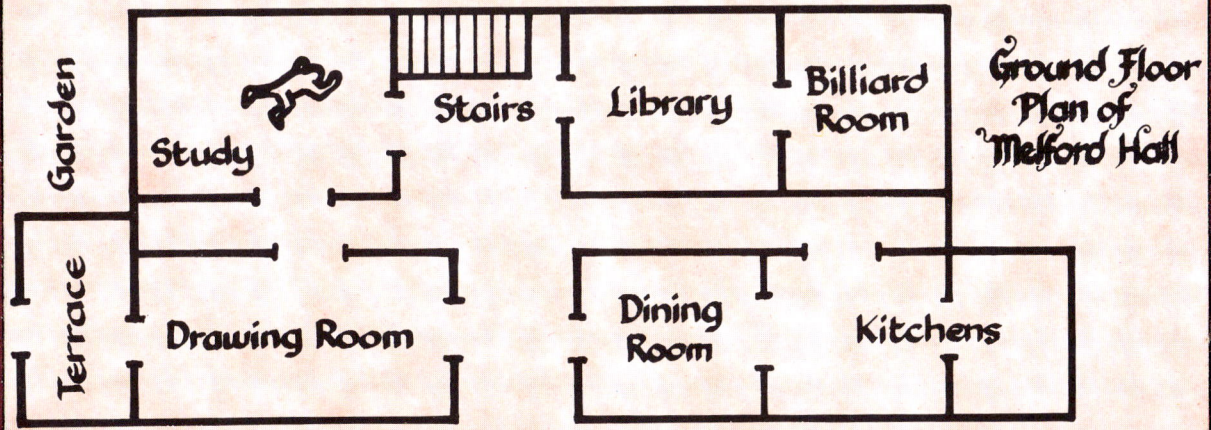

Garden

Study

Stairs

Library

Billiard Room

Ground Floor Plan of Melford Hall

Terrace

Drawing Room

Dining Room

Kitchens

Can you work out who killed the Colonel?

Turn to page 46 to see if you were right.

THE ELASTIC BAND

Mr. Trend has booked The Elastic Band to play at the Youth Club, but he can't remember which person plays what.

Can you help him? Look for the clues.

The Elastic Band were on the road again! They were in their van, driving to a concert. It was the first concert in their tour, so they were all a bit anxious.

'It's O.K. for you, Samantha,' said Chris. 'At least you don't have an instrument to worry about.'

'You can talk!' shouted Julie. 'You've only got four guitar strings to worry about — I've got six!'

The others laughed. But they still felt nervous. Mike had forgotten his cushion. He hoped he'd be able to find a comfortable chair to sit on while he played. You could tell Judi was nervous too. She kept tapping her drumsticks together in time with the windscreen wipers.

Two hours later they were on stage, ready to start.

Can you tell who is who in the picture? Write their names in the boxes.

INSTANT·YUK

It was **his** favourite food. **They** were **her** favourite, so when they met for tea they mixed them together! Yuk!

Who were the two people? What food did they mix together?

To find out, you'll need a dice.

To find out what **It** is, shake the dice. Look in the **blue** box. If you get a one [•] , you get honey. If you get a three [•••] ,you get yoghurt, and so on.

*Now shake the dice to find out who **he** is (red box), what **they** are (green box) and who **she** is (yellow box). You should get some lovely mixtures.*

IT (blue box)
- HONEY
- CUSTARD
- YOGHURT
- CHOCOLATE MOUSSE
- RHUBARB CRUMBLE
- STRAWBERRY JAM

HIS (red box)
- DRACULA'S
- PRINCE ANDREW'S
- GARGOYLE'S
- GRANDAD'S
- SHERLOCK ___'S
- THE HE___ER'S

THEY (green box)
- SAUSAGES
- CRISPS
- SALTED PEANUTS
- BEEF BURGERS
- FRIED EGGS
- BACON SANDWICHES

HER (yellow box)
- MRS. TH___ER'S
- ELSIE'S
- MUM'S
- FLORENCE NIGHTINGALE'S
- PRINCESS DI'S
- SUPERWOMAN'S

It, his, they and her are all pronouns. You could do this again, making up your own words to replace the pronouns.

31

THE SHERWOOD FOREST CLARION

THE HOOD GANG STRIKE AGAIN!

Another terrifying robbery took place in Sherwood Forest yesterday. Local people are reported to be scared to death as the area's crime rate soars. An elderly lady told our reporter, 'I never go through the forest now — it's much too dangerous.'

A shaken landowner, Mr. John King, was set upon by a group of thieves. 'There were lots of them, and they all wore green. Really vicious they were too — they threatened me with their bows and arrows. I saw a woman among them — a nasty piece of work. And there was an ugly fat monk as well. You can't trust anyone these days, can you? I never thought I'd get out alive. They took everything I have. Left me for dead, they did.'

Luckily for Mr. King, a passing jogger found him lying in the ditch and sent for help. Mr. King spent some time in the local hospital, and is now resting at home.

Officers from the Sheriff's Investigation Department are combing the forest, looking for evidence. The Sheriff himself made it clear he suspected the notorious Hood Gang, who have been operating in the forest for over a year.

'We'll bring these villains to justice soon — and then decent people will be able to live their lives without fear,' the Sheriff said to our reporter.

These two reports both tell the same story, but the points of view are very different. *Which newspaper do you think each of these people prefers to read? Write 'Clarion' or 'Badger' on each newspaper.*

The Badger

"The voice of the forest community!"

THREE CHEERS FOR THE HOOD GANG!

The latest daring exploit of the Hood Gang has thrilled the residents of Sherwood Forest. Landowner John King was set upon yesterday and was robbed of everything he had.

Many local people said that they had no pity for Mr. King. 'He's been robbing us for years,' said one local woman, Mrs. Beechnut. 'He charges high rents and makes our lives a misery. It's time he got a bit of his own medicine.'

Mr. King was found by local man, Bill Crabtree. 'I found him shaking in the ditch while I was out for my evening jog. He didn't seem to be hurt. The Sheriff's men took him to the hospital – I think he was just treated for shock.' Mr. King is now reported to be resting at home.

The description Mr. King gave to the Sheriff of his attackers talks of a large group of people, all dressed in green. They included a woman and a monk. Local people have no doubt that the Hood Gang were responsible for this exploit. The Gang have been operating in the forest for the past year. They choose their victims carefully, picking on the rich – they usually hand over the money they take to the poor people in the forest community.

The Sheriff's men are known to be hunting for the gang, but it is thought they will get little help from the local people.

Bits of books

The editor has to match the 6 book titles and illustrations with the 6 passages. *Can you write the title of the book above each passage?* You'll find the answers on page 46.

EDITOR

Oh no! Who left the window open?

Escape

Revenge.

The meeting

The bramble thicket

The Axe.

The Storm.

34

1   The track was very narrow. On either side the brambles and blackthorn tore at their legs and clothes. They had to keep moving. This was the only way out. The Thing was getting nearer. The birds in the thicket above them were silent.

2   They stood around the camp fire tense, alert, waiting. Then Olaf spoke. He held his axe high above his head. 'Come,' he said, 'it is time. We will avenge our brothers. The boat is ready. Let each man take up his axe and follow me.'

3   The only sound she could hear was the roar of the surf as it pounded onto the stony beach. She watched as the swell pulled back, dragging the sand and shingle with it. Again and again the waves returned with new fury, dashing against that desolate stretch of beach. She sat quite still, waiting, wondering. Would they come? Was this the place?

4   The man picked up the axe. It was strong and solid. The handle had been worn smooth by many hands before his. It felt good to hold. He skilfully sharpened the edge of the blade. The tiny flakes of flint shot away. Soon it would be ready to use again. With it he would chop wood for shelter and fuel for his fire.

5   The old men and women stood on the beach. The surf drenched their clothes. The spray lashed their faces. They did not turn away. Each one stood silently staring out to sea, hoping, praying, watching for a tiny blue and white speck on the horizon. Would the lifeboat bring their menfolk safely home? Or had they all perished?

6   She lay there panting, exhausted. Her soft grey sides heaved gently in and out. Her whole body trembled. She could go no further. She felt safe for a moment, hidden in that dense thicket. Somewhere above the brambles a blackbird was singing in the late autumn sunlight.

Gus and Hatchet and the chewing gum factory

TCHUMORA CHEWING GUM FACTORY

Gus and Hatchet are in a foreign city. This city has a factory which makes the best chewing gum in the world. The two villains are planning to break in and steal 29 packets. They hope to sell these for a high price in their stolen goods shop. It will not be easy — the gates of the factory are guarded by a soldier.

....

....

....

....

....

....

....

....

Gus is disguised as an artist. He is sitting in the park, just outside the factory, pretending to draw in his sketch book. Really he is trying to learn the picture code which he and Hatchet have agreed to use.

These are the pictures:

Here are the words. Can you write the correct word under each picture?

chewing gum
quiet
danger
sandwich

soldier
poison
look
sock

Hatchet comes to find Gus. As he approaches the soldier comes to sit on the bench by the side of Gus, and begins to eat his sandwiches. Gus quickly draws a message for Hatchet. This is what he draws:

Hatchet grabs the sketch book and draws this reply.

What do you think Gus and Hatchet are planning to do?

Can you write this message in picture code? You'll need to make up some pictures.

Danger! The sandwich is poisoned. Put a sock on the mouth of the dog.

POISON

37

THE HAUNTING OF HIRAM C. HOPGOOD

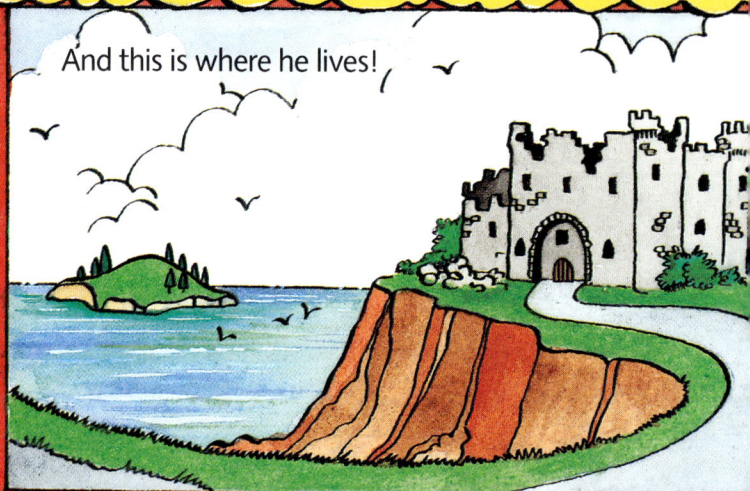

This is Alex . . .

And this is where he lives!

Alex is Laird of Carra, and Carra Castle is his home. But the castle is falling down and Alex has no money to repair it.

And so one day . . .

I have thought and I have thought and I have thought and I have decided to sell the castle.

I'm sure you're right, dear.

And so . . .

THIS CASTLE IS FOR SALE

After this nothing happened for a long time until one day a Mr. Hiram C. Hopgood, an American millionaire, came to see the castle.

THIS CASTLE IS FOR SALE

Alex just had time to change into his kilt before he showed Mr. Hopgood around.

Mr. Hopgood seemed to be pleased with what he saw.

I don't mind telling you, Alex, that I like this castle. I like it very much.

You can keep the little island. It's the castle I want. It's in a pretty ropey condition so all I'm prepared to offer is half a million pounds. Would that be acceptable?

Yes, sir. Absolutely. It would be fine.

There's just one thing. I've got a little daughter and she's delicate. She mustn't have any shocks. I will buy your castle — but only if there are no ghosts!

It was one of the most difficult moments of Alex's life. For a full minute he couldn't speak at all. Then he looked Mr. Hopgood straight in the eyes.

I swear to you, sir, that the castle you'll be buying will be entirely free of ghosts.

The trouble was that the castle was full of ghosts!! They were Alex's friends. He called them to a meeting that night.

'Ghosts of Carra', said Alex, clearing his throat, 'I bring you bad news'.

Alex had prepared a speech, but now he found he couldn't go on. A lump came into his throat and he had to shut his eyes to keep in the sudden tears.

Some children are brought up by their parents, some are sent away to boarding school so that it is their teachers who help them to grow up. But Alex had been brought up largely by his ghosts.

And it was these ghosts that he was going to send away! No, thought Alex wretchedly, I can't . . . it's impossible.

But he had given his word to Mr. Hopgood. He had promised — and with a great effort he said:

'The Castle has been sold. To a gentleman from America. I'm afraid I . . . I have to ask you to go and live somewhere else'.

What will they do? Will they leave? Where can they go? To find out about their adventures read 'The haunting of Hiram C. Hopgood' by Eva Ibbotson.

You could try to find this in the library or ask your mum or dad if they will buy it for you at your local bookshop. You can cut out the bit about the book on this page and take it with you.

The haunting of
Hiram C. Hopgood
Eva Ibbotson 1987
Macmillan
Children's
Books

The TREASURE of DARK ISLAND

Captain Aldridge buried his treasure on Dark Island. He cut the map into nine pieces so nobody could find the treasure.

Can you put the map together again, using these clues? Some will help you, some won't.

The boat house is north of the lake.
There are five buildings on the island.
The mansion house is east of Little Creek.
The compass points are in the north-east corner.
The lake is very deep at the north end.
There is a smaller island off the west coast.
The church is the furthest building from the lighthouse.
The fort is in ruins.

Cut out the nine pieces and try to put the map together. When you've done that, see if you can follow the trail to the treasure:

Land at the creek on the east coast. Go west until you reach the lake, then turn right. Keep going until you reach the sea. Then turn left and walk along the coast. Walk past the first building and keep walking along the coast. The treasure is buried at the next building you come to.

Where is the treasure? Mark its position with a cross.

When you've done this, you could try putting the nine pieces of the map together in a different way. There are lots of ways of doing this. Then try to write some clues for somebody else so they can make your island just like you did. You could make up a treasure trail too!

Lake Wett

BIG CREEK
Boat House

Round Bay

Church
Far Point

Old Fort

Light House

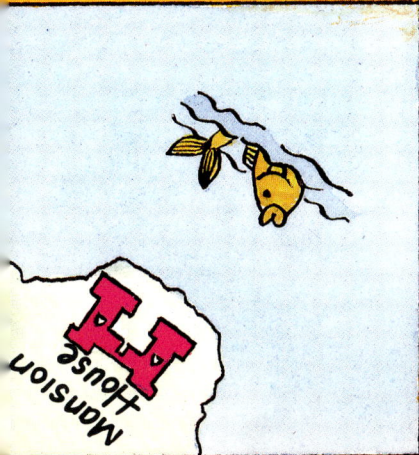
Mansion House

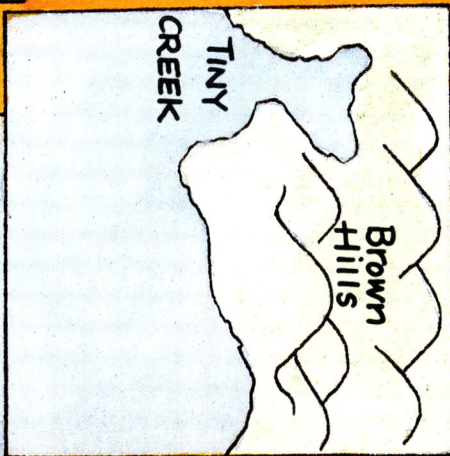
Tiny CREEK
Brown Hills

Little Creek

A PROVERB PUZZLE

Now what on earth is a proverb, Lisa?

A proverb is a sentence which says something which is true and which many people know and say. But a proverb says it in a funny way. We might say 'A bird in the hand is worth two in the bush' but we aren't really talking about birds. What we're really saying is that it's better to have one thing than to hope to have many things. Why don't you do this puzzle, then you'll see?

Here are some common proverbs, a picture for each and a list of possible meanings. **Can you draw lines to match the pictures and proverbs, and then between the proverb and the meaning you think is right?** *We've done the first one for you.*

It's funny, quite miss ...ish when ...e's not ...ound!

Dear Sid, Wish you were here. luv Trish

A stitch in time saves nine.	If a lot of people try to do something at the same time it won't get done properly.
Too many cooks spoil the broth.	It doesn't do any good to get upset once the damage has been done.
It's no good crying over spilt milk.	If you really want something, it's better to try to get it quickly.
Absence makes the heart grow fonder.	It's better to repair something quickly before the damage gets worse.
The early bird catches the worm.	We often feel more affection for someone when they are away, than when they are around all the time.

43

Skulk and Gargoyle clean out the cupboards

Skulk and Gargoyle are cleaning out the kitchen cupboards in the Ghoul End Guest House before the new lot of ghoul guests arrive.

> Look what I've found Gargoyle! Our favourite - let's have some for breakfast!

> Delicious - and we could have some of this to start with.

Sea slug Casserole

Serving Suggestion

Ingredients: Slug oil, Minced Gristle, Mud flavouring, Salt, Mould, Colour, (E101) Preservatives (E220, E221, E26407) Sodium Polyphosphate.

Made in Ghoulania

INSTANT SLIME SOUP

Full of vitamin
Tastes Foul!
Looks Foul!

Serving Suggestion

Ingredients: Slime extract, Fungi, lump enhancer, Flavouring — (monosodium glutamate), Grou rats' tails, Suga Stabiliser (435) Best bat fat.

Cooking Instructions

1 Empty contents into bucket.
2 Mix in 5 gallons of bog water.
3 Bring to boil - do not stir.
4 Simmer for 19 hours until required lumpy consistency.

Can you fill in the label for this bottle of squash?

Toad Spittle Squash

Ingredients. . . . .

Preparation. . . . .

Best Before. . . . .

Now find four tins or packets of food from your own cupboards. Choose two that you really like, and two that you can't stand. Look at the information on the labels and see if you can fill in a chart like the one below.

We've filled in the information on Seaslug Casserole to give you the idea:

BEST BEFORE OCT. 1967

	Seaslug Casserole				
How many ingredients does it contain?	10				
Does it contain fat?	NO				
Does it contain sugar?	NO				
Does it contain flavouring?	YES				
Does it contain colouring?	YES				
Does it contain preservatives?	YES				

Can you think of FOUR other things which food labels tell you?

ANSWER PAGE

The Cheat

Here are all the mistakes.
Did you find them in time?

There are 13 mistakes in Weedy's poem. Did you find them all?

The cheat

In 1904 the olympic Games were held in St. Louis, U.S.A. It was the day of the marathon. Among the runners an American called fred Lorz. The runners in this race have to cover 26 miles though the town and country before they finish in the stadium itself. it was very hot. The runners found hard going. Of the 31 entries 17 dropped dropped out. Fred Lorz exhausted. He dropped out after 14 kilometres The rest carried on.

Their was excitement in the stadium. The winner have been sighted. As he came onto the Track the crowd yelled with delight. He wore the the colours of U.S.A. It was Fred Lorz!

How had he done it The crafty Fred had hitched a lift in a car. The truth soon came out out and Fred was disqualified. Fortunately for the Americans another of there countrymen came next so they got the gold after all! it still must have taken some time to get over the shame of Fred!

MURDER AT MELFORD HALL

Emma Seaton is the murderer. She lied about going upstairs to fetch her sweater. Instead she went into the study and poisoned the Colonel.

WHO'S WHO?

 1. Mr. U    2. Sid Genius

 3. Gus    4. Tatty Tricia    5. Gargoyle    6. Feetman    7. Maud    8. Cannibal

 9. Hatchet    10. Elsie    11. Skulk    12. Paul    13. Myrtle    14. Weedy Weasel

FIND THE FLAGS

NETHERLANDS   MONACO   COLOMBIA

INDONESIA   AUSTRIA   SPAIN

Bits of books

The correct titles for the passages are:

1. Escape
2. Revenge
3. The Meeting
4. The Axe
5. The Storm
6. The Bramble Thicket

the Success! AWARDS CEREMONY

And now – ladies and gentlemen. The success awards ceremony!

Be the judge and give these famous awards to the pages you thought were best. Write in the names of the activities you choose on the lines.

I give the MAUD'S LETTER WRITING AWARD to the activity I enjoyed the most.

This was ....

I give the PAUL SWEATSHIRT AWARD to the activity I did best.

This was ....

I give the WEEDY WEASEL TEETH AWARD to the activity I thought was the funniest.

This was ....

But I give the HATCHET CHEWED GUM AWARD to the activity I thought was the worst.

This was ....

I didn't like this one because ....

Try to give a reason. Was it really boring? Was it not funny? Was it too hard?

U.S.A

SUCCESS!

means GREATIDEAS

> **❝** *The very best educational process lies in a confident partnership between child, parents and teachers.* **❞**

Success! gives you the chance to make your contribution as effective as possible. We provide a range of imaginative opportunities for you to select from. They can be combined in different ways to achieve the progress you are looking for.

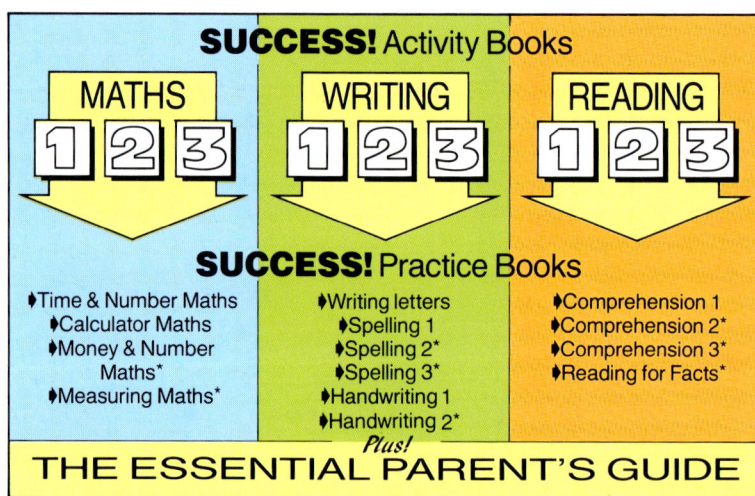

SUCCESS! Activity Books

MATHS	WRITING	READING
1 2 3	1 2 3	1 2 3

SUCCESS! Practice Books

◆Time & Number Maths	◆Writing letters	◆Comprehension 1
◆Calculator Maths	◆Spelling 1	◆Comprehension 2*
◆Money & Number Maths*	◆Spelling 2*	◆Comprehension 3*
◆Measuring Maths*	◆Spelling 3*	◆Reading for Facts*
	◆Handwriting 1	
	◆Handwriting 2*	

Plus!

THE ESSENTIAL PARENT'S GUIDE

* in preparation

SUCCESS! *activity books*

This book is only one of nine activity books covering Maths, Writing and Reading. These books provide challenging and attractive exercises in the *whole business* of the main subjects.

You can choose the subject or subjects that you think particularly need help, and start with the first Level in each one to see how much progress can be made.

SUCCESS! *practice books*

This is a series of books designed to improve specific skills which are part of the whole business of each subject. The exercises are easier than the Activity Books, but they are still lots of fun to do. They concentrate on building ability and confidence in the basic tools everyone needs to be good at the subjects.